JESU, JOY OF MAN'S DESIRING

(from Cantata No. 147)

Transcribed by
RICK FOSTER

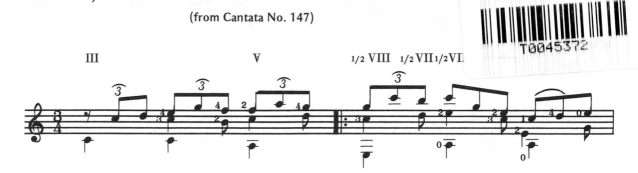

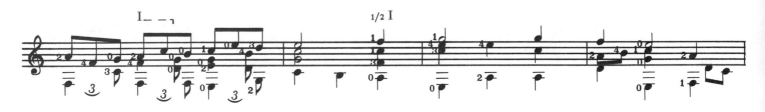

PRELUDE No. I

(Well-Tempered Clavier)

Transcribed for Guitar by
CHRISTOPHER PARKENING

J.S. BACH

Tune the 6th string to "D"

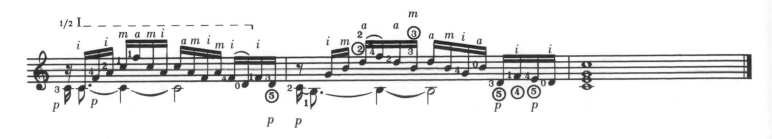

PRELUDE No. VI

(Well-Tempered Clavier)

Transcribed for Guitar by
CHRISTOPHER PARKENING

J.S. BACH

Tune the 6th string to "D"

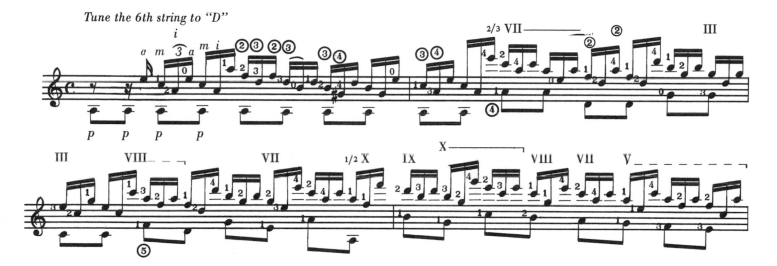

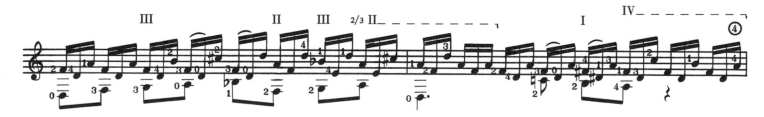

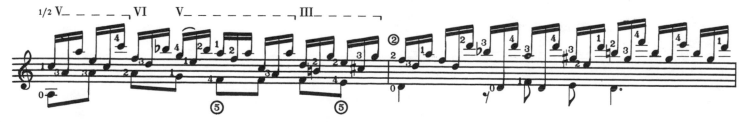

PRELUDE No. IX

(Well-Tempered Clavier)

Transcribed for Guitar by
KRES AMELOTTE

J.S. BACH

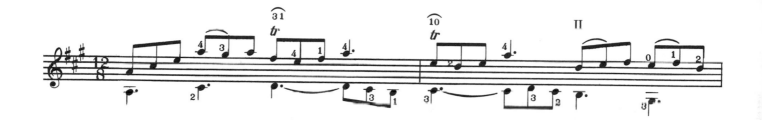

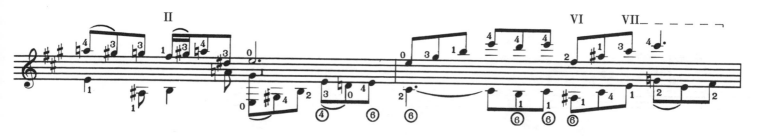

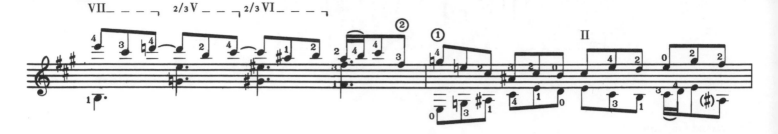

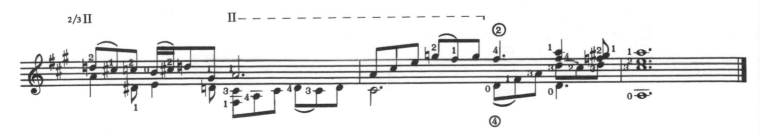

SHEEP MAY SAFELY GRAZE

(from Cantata No. 208)

What I allude to in left hand technique as the "double bar" or "cross fret bar" is utilized in the following piece by Bach. In this "double bar," the index finger bars across two adjacent frets simultaneously. The bottom half of the index finger depresses the 1st, 2nd, and 3rd (treble) strings on the lower-sounding fret. The top half of the index finger depresses the 4th, 5th, and 6th (bass) strings on the higher-sounding fret. I have notated this by showing the two frets with a slash line between them. If, for example, the eight and ninth frets are to be barred with the index finger, the notation is as follows: VIII/IX.

Transcribed by
RICK FOSTER

J.S. BACH

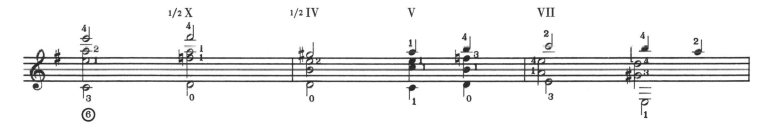

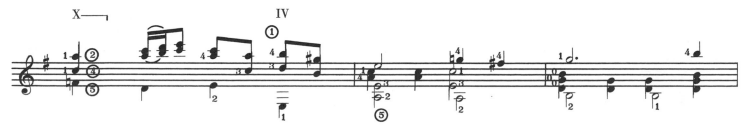

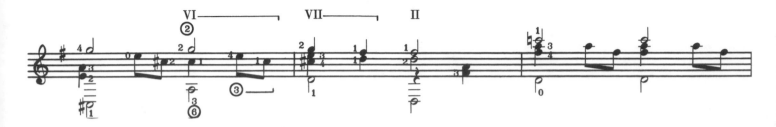

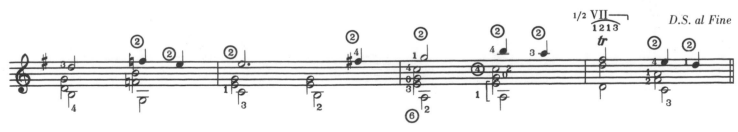

SLEEPERS, AWAKE!

(from Cantata No. 140)

Transcribed by
CHRISTOPHER PARKENING

J.S. BACH

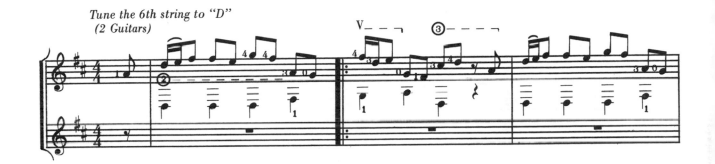

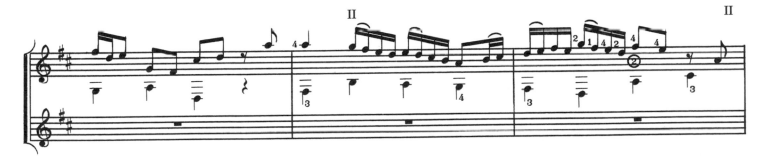

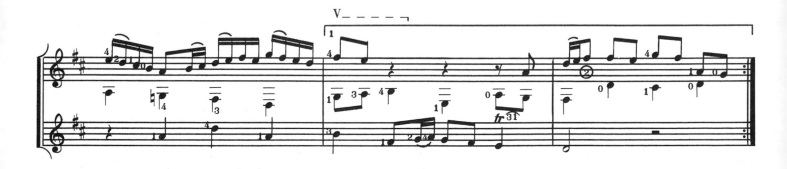

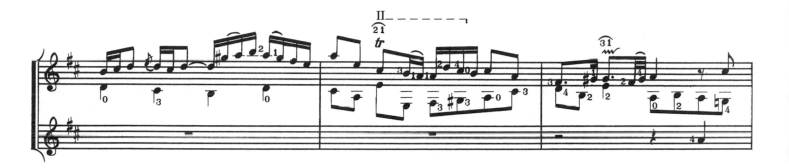

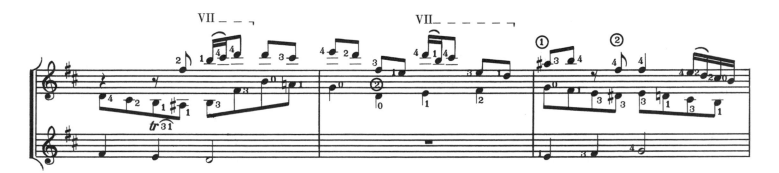

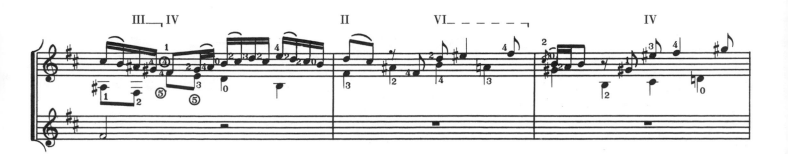

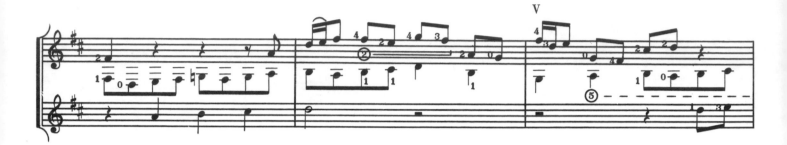

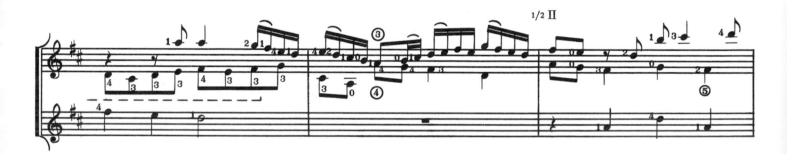

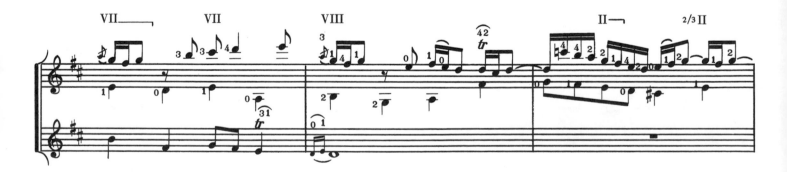

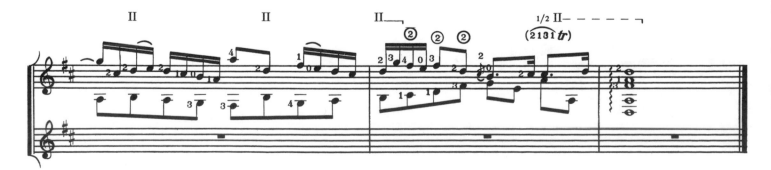

BE THOU WITH ME

Transcribed by
JERROLD HYMAN

J.S. BACH

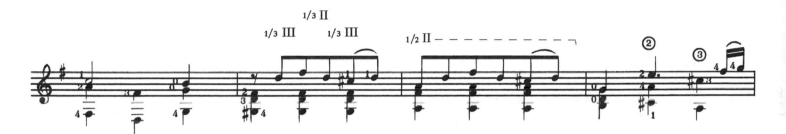

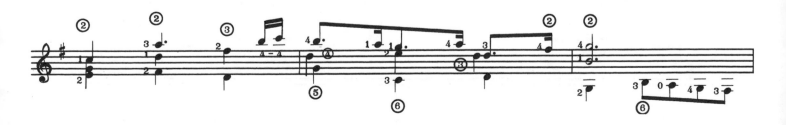

GAVOTTE I & II

(from 5th Cello Suite)

I

Transcribed for Guitar by
CHRISTOPHER PARKENING

J.S. BACH

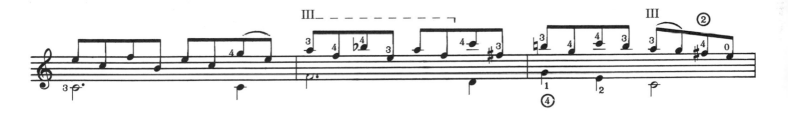

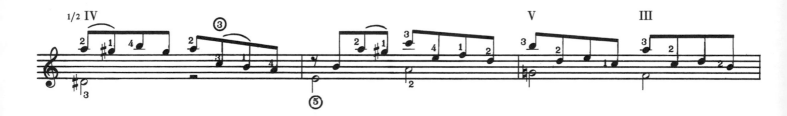

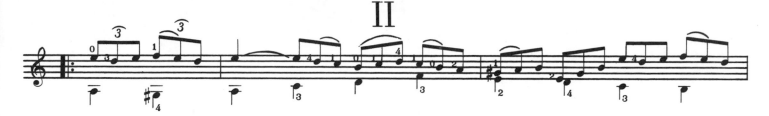

II

Gavotte I - *D.C.*

PRELUDE

Transcribed by
JERROLD HYMAN

J.S. BACH

ALTERNATE FINGERING & NOTATION

Arranged by
JERROLD HYMAN and JAMES F. SMITH

24